Perspectives
A View of My Own

I0117952

Barbara Arner

chipmunkapublishing
the mental health publisher

Published by
Chipmunkapublishing
PO Box 6872
Brentwood
Essex CM13 1ZT
United Kingdom

http://www.chipmunkapublishing.com

Edited by Lucy Lythgoe

ISBN   978-1-84991-667-7

Chipmunkapublishing   gratefully   acknowledge   the support of Arts Council England.

For my parents
Thank you for giving me life.

Barbara Arner

Contents

When you are joyous, look deep into your heart, and you shall find it is only that which has given you sorrow that is giving you joy. When you are sorrowful, look again in your heart, and you shall see that in truth you are weeping for that which has been your delight.

-Khalil Gibran

We don't see things as they are; we see them as we are.

-Anais Nin

Barbara Arner

Barbara Arner

1. The Depressed

Every time it happens, I think, "Life's not fair. I know that, I've learned that" and then it comes, usually out of nowhere, but it comes like a tidal wave and screws up everything: the happiness, the diet, the exercise regime, and the relationships. I can't shower. I only want to sleep, stay in bed, and wonder why. Then the suicidal thoughts happen: "I don't want to live like this anymore. Why do I have to suffer from this illness? It's not fair."

And so bipolar disorder goes on. Life goes on. I take my medication, see my psychiatrist, and continue to experience reoccurring depressions. Feeling emotional pain and wanting to die, for it all to end, but I stay. My mom would miss me. Who would take care of my cat and dog? My mom would have to clean out all my shit: all that artwork, the enormous kiln, the heavy potter's wheel, the shelves, buckets of glaze, glaze chemicals, all that clay. I couldn't do that to her, so I stay, depressed, wanting to go, but I stay.

My mom loves me. She manages to stay as well, taking care of me when I can't take care of myself. She tells me I'm beautiful, that so many people love me, and she listens to every word I have to say. I couldn't leave her. I don't want to. I just don't want to feel this way anymore—too much shit.

If you have bipolar disorder, you get it. If you don't, you're lucky. Your life is not a reoccurring nightmare like mine with unpredictable mood swings: feeling depressed and manic over and over again. Give me a break already. The body and mind get exhausted from this process. How strong do I have to be? But I remember, or try to remind myself, the depression does pass and I will feel better in time: patience. If you have bipolar disorder and this is not your experience and you feel pretty good all the time, then consider yourself lucky, blessed, fortunate, but I just can't seem to get there all the time. Who is happy when they can't physically move, get out of bed, go to the gym, go to work, and wants to have the ice cream as opposed to choosing the apple? Fuck you, illness. I hate you.

My mom would miss me and I'd hate to leave her with all my shit. I'd also hate to leave the only life I was given; that was chosen for me; that I was fated. I'd hate to lose, lose the fight—the stupid mind-fuck of a fight to a mental illness yet people do. Supposedly every sixteen minutes someone dies to suicide. I really don't want to be a statistic—too much shit. Too much shit I've been through. So I remain optimistic. I will get better. The sun will shine. The depression will pass. My psychiatrist keeps me company and he gets it. He keeps me alive over and over again, time and time again. He should be a millionaire by now having to deal with all my shit, and he does, kindly and patiently, he does.

People usually get depressed because of something: the death of a parent, a bad relationship, some weight gain, an illness. I have gotten depressed for all these reasons and it sucks. You feel awful, but the truth is it passes. You have fond memories of your loved one, you say goodbye to the bad relationship, and you eat healthy and exercise. It passes, you go on. These are the easy depressions. The mental illness of bipolar disorder has a life of its own. It creeps up on you whenever it wants. It's not fair. You learn that each time. Life is not fair and you fight yet again to stay alive.

You look around at people living. They go to work, they have the house, the family, the life they wanted, they willingly created. They can fucking shower. They are living and I am here in bed. I want to get out, but I can't so I close my eyes and bury myself in blankets with my cat and dog snuggled close to me and we sleep. The sane mind says, "Get out of bed, shower, eat something healthy, take the dog for a walk, go to the gym, see a friend, just get up and go." If it were that fucking easy there would be no bipolar disorder. I would function. I would have a job, the kids, the house, everything—medication would work all the time—but the illness lingers on. But at least I'm not manic, not delusional: I'm depressed. I know you depression and I hate you. Fuck you, depression. You have made my life a living hell. Just go away forever. Let me live my life in peace. Let my mom have a break from having a sick child. Give me a break. Stop making my psychiatrist work so hard. Please stop killing me. So the disability money gets deposited and I deal. I feel like a complete failure. "But she was so nice, so talented." Well, she was. Fuck you, illness. Why me? Life is not fair.

My parents are not to blame. They put so much energy into properly raising my sister, brother, and me: good schools, healthy activities, good friends, no drugs. I never even smoked a cigarette. I really didn't fuck up or deserve you, illness. I really didn't. Fuck you. My siblings aren't to blame either. They are simply going about their lives living the best they can. I want the barking dog, the screaming child, the stressful job that pays: livable chaos. Instead, I have a life that has been filled with tears and anger. It's really not fair.

Barbara Arner

2. The Patient

I usually prefer the packaged food for breakfast. I choose the cereal box with a carton of skim milk, a container of yogurt, and juice. I choose orange juice, but they have others as well: grapefruit, cranberry, apple. The hot breakfasts of pancakes, French toast, or eggs scare me. They are usually cold anyway. So raisin bran works just fine for me in the Styrofoam bowl with a plastic spoon. It's all placed on a tray with my name and menu attached and another blank menu to fill out for tomorrow's glorious breakfast. Yes, the next day. Does there have to be another fucking day in this place? And getting out takes forever: going to therapy groups, meeting with the psychiatrist, only to ask over and over again, "when do I get to go home?", sleeping in beds with rock-hard mattresses, showering in stalls used by others, not being able to use a razor. But shave? Me, shave? I can't even get out of bed. I'm depressed and I am here again.

Everyone experiences the psychiatric hospital differently. Some have good experiences, others have not. I fit into the latter category. I just don't like being locked in some place trying to get better and trying to get out. Because the truth is you do not get better. Maybe temporarily, but it returns. Only to be depressed again, suicidal, and then hospitalized: contained and painfully observed.

As I've gotten older throughout the past fifteen years since my diagnosis, I've been hospitalized less, but the feeling of being there, the memories live on. They live inside you, you can feel them, and it's not fun.

So I choose cereal and get on with the day. If I'm feeling better, by maybe day two or three, I have showered. They have soap used as both a body wash and shampoo—no conditioner. After all, this is a mental hospital not the Hilton. No razors allowed. When you finish showering in a stall that everyone uses you get out making sure only to step on the clean towel placed on the floor, gross germs lingering. You take your clean clothes off the contaminated surfaces and dress. You walk out knowing you have a roommate around somewhere. You have to ask for a blow dryer, but since that requires effort you leave with your hair wet. In a timely manner you start the day: breakfast, therapy groups, a group on medication, a recreational therapy group, and, if you're lucky, they will let you outside and you can breathe in fresh air. It all sucks. I want the barking dog, the unruly child, the job that pays, but I am stuck in here only to be greeted during visiting hours by my confused, hurt family. They try to make me feel better, but then they have to leave, say goodbye, walk off the locked ward, and, hopefully, return tomorrow.

And so I behave and hope to get the fuck out. Except for one time—I screamed, yelled in anger and frustration, so they attacked me. They put me in one of those quiet rooms and shot me in the ass with something. It didn't help; it just made my life worse and made me feel angrier. Why couldn't someone have just talked to me, asked me why I was so angry, asked me what happened—listened. But, no, attacked and shot in the ass. I must be a terrible person. Fuck you, terrible illness. Fuck you for making me feel so angry, so hurt, so discontent, so... depressed.

So I prefer to stay in my own bed. Suicidal or not, I want to be home. My animals keep me company, my mom visits me, and I don't have to have their breakfasts. I can watch TV anytime I want to, I can even go outside anytime. I can take my own medication without someone watching me. I can shower when I'm ready in my own shower. I can be alone. Thank you, psychiatrist, for trusting me and keeping me out of those places. I'm not locked in, checked in, only wanting to be checked out over and over again. It's an awful feeling, an awful experience—for me, anyway.

Maybe it will take a few days for the depression to pass, a few months, years, or maybe it will take just a few seconds, but it passes and the flip side you are left to cope with is even worse: mania.

Barbara Arner

Barbara Arner

3. The Manic

The cup is half full. You have energy, you are happy. You're getting things done, you're out of bed, and, yes, showering and shaving for that matter. You are smiling. You're feeling great. Life couldn't be better. Okay, so maybe the cup may be overflowing quite a bit, well, pouring out, unable to contain anything. Then it gets crazy, a mess, only to be locked up again.

Welcome to mania. Fuck you, illness, for screwing up my life yet again. I am just trying to live. True manic episodes are a terrible experience. They wreak havoc, mad chaos upon your life. There is no sense, no fulfillment, and no happiness. You may speak a mile a minute trying to keep up with a racing mind, you may spend excessive amounts of money leaving you financially screwed, you may ruin relationships, and you may even die. It's not fun, and, mania, I don't want any part of you. It is dangerous and unsafe and only leaves you bitter, sad, and resentful that yet again something negative had to happen.

My first manic episode left me handcuffed, strapped to a stretcher, hospitalized, and, yes, diagnosed. "You have bipolar disorder," said the hippie doctor sitting on the counter in the Vermont hospital. Yeah, I know. I've known since high school, but I just haven't said anything. Now the whole world knows or so it seems.

I was in my second year of college, nineteen years old, when I lost my mind for the first time. Things were going so well. I was an honor student, a resident assistant for the first year students on my dorm room floor, I was biking, skiing, had nice friends, classes were interesting and productive. I was studying art and psychology. Yes, psychology: fascinated by the human brain, fascinated by my brain, by my fluctuating moods of bipolar disorder. It was my secret. I knew I had this illness and I was reading everything about it.

I read about bipolar disorder for the first time in high school. I was in the school library digging through books on depression trying to find an answer on how to feel better. I read about this thing called "bipolar disorder" and got scared because it sounded exactly like me with my unpredictable, fluctuating moods. I quickly put the book back on the shelf and got the hell out. I didn't want any part of this illness. I wanted to be normal. I didn't want an illness that may end in suicide. I was scared. I didn't want to have this in my lifetime so I got the hell out. That was high school and then came college with the full-blown manic episode.

Everything happened so fast. My mind was racing—I thought I was going to conquer the world. I was talking out in class, even jumped on a stage during a class defending some sort of nonsensical idea. My professors were concerned. One evening they sent counselors to my dorm room. I was angry. This was not supposed to be happening to me. I'm a good person, a great friend, a good student—what was going on here? The counselors called the police because I would not open my door. I was officially insane. I ran out of my room, the cops chased me, cornered me, handcuffed me, and the paramedics put me on a stretcher and into the ambulance. I went to the hospital and was then diagnosed by the hippie doctor reconfirming my previous findings. I had to leave school and return back to New Jersey. Fuck you, illness, for screwing up my life.

I've had other psychotic, delusional manic episodes since, but I think I've lost track and really don't care to remember. Medication sometimes works, sometimes it doesn't. I get hospitalized and then left to cope with an impossible, unfair illness again. It sucks. And then I get depressed because of everything. This is the never-ending, exhausting cycle of bipolar disorder.

Barbara Arner

4. The Ski Instructor

I've always loved skiing. The quick, mad rush of flying down a mountain is exhilarating and addictive—over and over again since I was seven. Three years ago, I went to a ski resort in New Jersey to finally ski for the day.

An instructor at Mountain Creek saw me skiing and mentioned instructing. I was open to the idea so he led me to another instructor who skied with me. I guess they thought I was good enough because I was invited to instruct. Fun, I thought. This should be fun. Wow—fun—a new concept in my fucked up life, and, even better, it was a job I could do. It was skiing! I might be out of my mind, but I can ski. And I did—successfully instructing at Mountain Creek for the past three years.

I moved up to a small town in New Jersey to be close to my new, fun job. My parents were supportive helping me rent a house and I was ready to begin. I was finally working again, and, better yet, I was doing something I loved. It felt great. I learned so much that first year: how to instruct, how to ski better. I was surrounded by so many nice people and it was so much fun. Finally something I enjoyed; something I loved; something I could do.

The previous year I had treated myself to new skis and boots, but I didn't use them. Lift tickets are expensive and I was not working due to my illness. So the new skis and boots just sat there for a year. The pretty white skis and boots just sat there looking at me. I was finally going to be using them and often. I was happy.

I credit some of my happiness in my life to Mountain Creek. So, thank you, my dear Mountain. Thank you for giving me such nice people in my life and thank you for employing me, bipolar and all.

For the past three winters, I have been able to ski my heart out. Not only have my co-workers made me happier, but my students have brought a lot of happiness into my life. I have taught children as young as three years old how to ski. I have never experienced so many smiles and thank yous in my life. Bipolar and all, you are all very welcome. Thank You.

Since my second year instructing, I have managed to get my Level 1 certification from the Professional Ski Instructors of America. I have even been able to purchase a new pair of boots replacing my beginner boots. I was advancing in something and it was skiing and it was fun. The most exhilarating sport I have experienced and it felt really good. And, even better, it was an activity that would keep me healthy, keep me physically in shape, and force me to take better care of myself to be able to perform better. And, each year, I have gotten better. I've improved with instructing and improved with skiing. In the bright, shining sun, snow, sleet, rain, and freezing cold it has been fun.

One of my memorable experiences at Mountain Creek was teaching my nephew, Charlie, how to ski. Charlie is four years old and my sister's son. Everyone loves Charlie. He is the sweetest child I know and to be with him is pure joy.

My sister, my mother, and Charlie met me on a quiet Monday up at Mountain Creek. It was beautifully sunny and we were all smiles. Finally, I was going to teach Charlie how to ski and he was excited. We all were.

First, the boots—he looked uncomfortable and strange to the idea of ski boots. Then the little skis came. I think he was skeptical of this whole process. He looked adorable with his little helmet and goggles on and we were ready to go.

We walked up to the School Yard where beginners learn to ski. Skis off we started with boots drills. He was bored. Then we put one ski on to gradually progress to two. We skied in a circle with one ski on, but he wanted both immediately. Skiing enthusiasm—I love it. So we put on two skis and started skiing on the flats. He wanted to go up the hill—fearless. Within minutes we were going up the Magic Carpet, a conveyor belt that brings you to the top of the hill. I was thrilled with his eagerness to ski. Everything was going so well. We got up to the top and I was explaining skiing in a wedge and parallel skiing, otherwise known to children as "pizza" and "French fries." He just wanted to go and so we did. And while we were skiing down he asked me in his little voice, "Will you come over to my house for a couple minutes?" Confirmation: he loved me.

I taught Charlie how to ski that day and we were all happy. He learned and he was thrilled with his new sport. I was thrilled. Thank you, Mountain Creek, for making us all happy.

A ski lesson that brings happiness to both the instructor and student is priceless. Everyone has a good time and smiles abound. Charlie was happy, my sister was happy, my mother was, and I was. It was a great day at Mountain Creek sunshine and all.

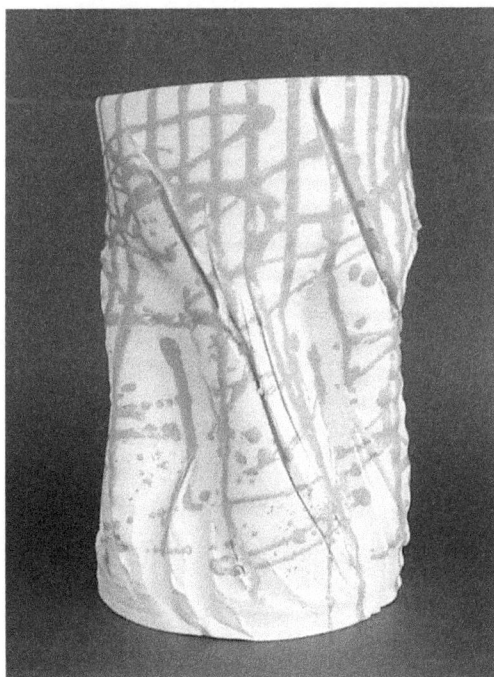

Barbara Arner

5. The Artist

After breakdown #1 in college, I stayed at home for a semester, attended a nearby college, and then returned to University of Vermont. I was determined to finish my education at the place where I started regardless of my setbacks. I did not want to be left behind from my classmates. Thankfully, my parents were supportive of my decision to return to Vermont.

For my junior year, I went to classes for the fall semester back at UVM. It was strange being back after getting sick, but comfortable and familiar at the same time. I saw the University's psychiatrist and counseling center for the remainder of my education. I was getting through and they were willing to help me and they did so ever so kindly.

I made it through the fall of junior year successfully and had a new wish: to study abroad in Italy for my spring semester. Once again, my parents were supportive of my plans. I applied to a program in Florence, Studio Art Centers International, to study art. When I was accepted, I packed my one suitcase for the semester and was eager to begin. I was happy again.

I stayed in Italy for three months and it was amazing. I had previously studied Italian so I had a sense of the language and since I was an art major I was ready to begin my classes. I chose to take a Renaissance art history class, drawing, interior design, and ceramics. I loved my art history class. Every weekend we traveled somewhere new to see beautiful architecture, museums, even the Coliseum. And, in my drawing class, I was recognized as the most improved so seeing my drawing skills evolve was very rewarding. In my interior design class, I designed a library which included making my first model. And, in my ceramics class, I fell in love: with clay. I had never worked in clay as a medium before; not even as I remember as a child.

We made various sculptures and then we were introduced to the potter's wheel.

I sat down, centered the clay, and made a form. The student next to me called me "a natural" and for the rest of the semester I used the potter's wheel every chance I could get. It was such a peaceful, calming process. My instructor complimented me and critiqued me and I loved it.

My trip to Italy concluded with a visit from my parents. It was one of the most memorable trips with my parents that I have. They arrived in Florence and I showed them around the city and then we moved on to Rome. My father, being an architect, was eager to explore and we saw all the sites. My parents even went to see the Pope say mass. Together we had a great time.

After finishing in Italy, I went to finish my education back in Vermont. One more year and then I would have accomplished my goal. I decided to finish with a degree in art and psychology. I concentrated on ceramics for the remainder of my education. I continued my passion of working on the potter's wheel and finished with a dinnerware set. I was pleased with my advancement.

My parents were supportive of my interests and after graduation they helped me purchase a potter's wheel and an electric kiln. I set up everything in my garage where I continue to work. I have had many exhibits and my art has been collected by many people. I love sharing my passion with others which has led me to instruct as a pottery teacher as well. I've worked in many pottery studios throughout New Jersey and have taught children ages four through adults. I can make my own glazes and clay and have explored many firing techniques in addition to my electric kiln. I've also taken other classes and workshops and this passion never seems to leave me. It only continues to be enhanced with every experience I have. I love developing new forms, new glazes, and seeing my work evolve. It is always very rewarding to see progress and to see art I have created myself.

Barbara Arner

Perspectives: A View of My Own

Barbara Arner

6. The Runner

Throughout my life, I have been involved with many athletic activities. These include swimming, basketball, soccer, tennis, softball, biking, running, and, of course, skiing. All these activities kept me very healthy. It was only until after I first got sick in my sophomore year of college that I had physical problems: weight gain.

As my mental health deteriorated, my physical health declined as well. Depressed, I no longer had the energy, motivation, or desire to take care of myself. I did not exercise and I opted to eat to cope when I was depressed. Twice I gained approximately fifty pounds. As my weight increased both times my desire to partake in any of these activities vanished. I was not even skiing. It was a losing battle. I'd stay in bed, eat, gain weight, not exercise, and continue to be depressed: an awful vicious cycle. Who can take care of themselves when they are feeling so depressed? At the time I was also on medicine that caused weight gain so that did not help my situation either. The choices I made were poor.

This time around and who I am today is different. I am more proactive with my health. I care. I care about my health and my life now. When you are depressed, you want to die. Ice cream and comfort foods temporarily made me feel better, but fifty pounds later, twice, makes you feel much worse. I refuse to fall into this pattern again.

The life I've created and who I am today is different. Yes, I still experience depressions, but I cope differently now. I choose not to eat and find other ways to comfort myself. The comfort foods are no longer an option. It will not, in the long run, make me feel good and it will not help me in coping with my illness.

I am fortunate I sought out a fitness club that was supportive with my weight loss efforts. They helped me to develop new habits of eating well and exercising.

For the past year, they have helped me achieve my fitness goals, and, once again, I am enjoying the activities I used to enjoy growing up. I am looking forward to the summer at the beach, swimsuit and all. I was able to have the most successful ski season in my third year due to my weight loss and improved fitness level. Everything is better when you are taking care of your physical self while trying your best to take care of your mental health. It is not easy. My diet has completely and permanently changed. I eat fruits and vegetables, protein, and carbohydrates daily. I have a healthy mindset as well. I no longer eat to cope when depressed. I take care of myself because this time around I really do care.

Barbara Arner

7. My Perspective

I'm in bed. It's 11 p.m. My dog is jumping on me, getting my attention. She needs to go out. It's dark and I think, "Can't you just wait until the morning?" but she is really jumping. So I collect my nerves and her leash and we go out. We move quietly and quickly. She pees. We're back in the house. The door is locked. I'm back in bed. I'm safe. She still hasn't settled down—still jumping getting my attention. She has to poop. Can't you wait until morning? So I put her leash on again as my heart beats. I hate this all with a passion, but I have to let her out again so we go. She poops and then we're back inside. Door locked we're both safe and alive. We made it.

I lived with this fear for a few years. I used to have panic attacks due to this anxiety which required hospitalizations, but within the past year I have not: making progress. My dog and I are alive. Cat, too. Mom, check. Siblings, check.

I moved to a small town in New Jersey before my first ski season. My family and I were very excited. I would not only be living on my own for the first time, I would be working. These are huge steps for some people with bipolar disorder: independence and a job.

The house I would be renting had one bedroom, a kitchen, living room, and family room. It had new carpet and was freshly painted. It was my ideal house. It really was. Small, affordable, and a house—all to myself! I was very excited.

My parents helped me move in. My dad willingly helped me move all my pottery equipment. I was making the back room my art studio. I had my potter's wheel, clay, shelves, and my wedging board. I was set. This was perfect. I decorated my bedroom with an abstract flower painting I had made for the matching comforter. In the bathroom, I had pottery for a soap dish, cup, toothbrush holder, tissue box, and wall hanging: deep maroon. I had, of course, matching towels all purchased from Macy's. My Macy collection continued into the kitchen with turquoise dish towels, place mats, and napkins. I also hung a blue abstract painting of a wave. My new Macy purchases continued with pots, pans, cups, and utensils. Where my Macy purchases finally ended, began my Ikea ones: my new cream colored couch, the two coffee tables, the dark wood table with cream colored chairs, and the island for the kitchen. I loved how I made this house a home. And, even better, this rented house was for sale! I was beginning my independent life and it felt great.

In addition to my ski job, I also had a job teaching ceramics at senior centers throughout New Jersey. I would travel to nearly a dozen centers, nursing homes, and hospitals with my clay cart sharing my passion. We made bowls, plates, vases, mugs, sculpture, and it was fun. It was something I could do and do well. I loved hearing the stories of the people I worked with: humorous, sad, and everything in between. And they were always so thrilled to see their finished masterpieces: fired, glazed, and beautiful. I loved this job. I even participated in a craft show and sold some of my own pottery in my new town. I liked my new hometown. I liked the salon where I went to get manicures and pedicures, the restaurants around the tranquil lake, its natural surroundings. I went for long walks and fast bike rides around my neighborhood. I was healthy. I was happy. I think that was where it all ended. That was three years ago.

I have two necklaces from my parents that hold sentimental value to me. One is gold with freshwater pearls that my parents gave me for Christmas when I was twelve. The other is silver with diamonds and a blue topaz stone. This was also given to me by my parents for Christmas when I was in my late 20s. My dad thought it was too expensive to buy, but my mom bought it anyway. Both of these necklaces made me think of my parents love towards me.

The guy who lived across from me in my new hometown was a little strange. The day I moved in he was over at my house introducing himself and me to the neighborhood. He seemed nice, not bad-looking either, but then he continued to come over often. He always offered to help out around my house. I continuously and politely declined his offers. I think his girlfriend was getting upset constantly having outbursts. Then one day when I was in my walk-out basement, he popped in, literally inside the basement, startling me. I was cornered. Nervous, I tried to stay calm. He was a sniper in the army and his sudden appearances scared me. He must have sensed my nerves. I wasn't comfortable at all with his advances. I got out of the walk-out basement quickly and declined another offer and went safely into my house. The next day I bought a lock for my basement and kept myself safe locking all the doors of the house all the time—except for once.

I went for a quick bike ride around the neighborhood and left my side door unlocked. I'm not sure why I did, I guess I thought I would be gone for a short amount of time. In the daylight it would be fine. I went for the bike ride. I had seen this sniper look out his window at my house a few times and it bothered me. As I approached my house on my bike, I saw him banging on my side door. "Hello? Hello?" I approached him, and, once again, was nervous that he was by my house. He told me that his girlfriend kicked him out and he was leaving. He wanted to say goodbye. I was glad he was leaving and would finally be leaving me alone. I wouldn't be scared anymore. He kissed my hand and said goodbye. I was disgusted. He left.

I went back into my unlocked house and looked around nervous that he had made his way in while I was biking. I looked for my necklace where I kept my jewelry and it was gone. An expensive piece of jewelry was missing. I thought just maybe I misplaced it, but I never put it anywhere else and he was by my door and it was unlocked. Makes sense, no?

Assuming theft, I went down to the police station to report a missing necklace. I was met by this young police officer and told to fill out a report. While I was writing about the incident he was busy drawing phallic symbols. I stared at it, he crumbled it up, and went out of the room. He returned with more paper for me. I was writing about the incident in detail. I was upset and thought my beautiful necklace from my parents was stolen. I had printed out a picture of a similar necklace from the web site showing the necklace and its value. This situation concluded by the police officer searching his house and finding nothing. Sniper boy was angry. You really don't want a sniper angry at you and now he was. I was already stressed and distraught over this necklace—now I had a sniper angry. I was dead.

I continued on feeling safe with this police department. My neighbors next to me said they were friends with the cops if there was ever a problem with this guy. It appeared they weren't very fond of him either. Apparently, he was heavily into drugs. I learned that my neighbor diagonally across the street from me was a police officer so I felt even safer from the intrusive sniper. Everything was going to be alright, right? No. Not at all.

This police officer across the street from me never said "hello" and did not strike me as a friendly neighbor. He was always working on his house or car with his back towards me. I did a lot of my pottery work outside my house. Whether it was throwing on my potter's wheel on the side porch, recycling clay in the front of the house, or mixing chemicals for glazes in my walk-out basement I was constantly outside. I felt like my neighbors were naturally curious about my artistic lifestyle or maybe they just didn't give a shit, but I always caught glances whenever they neared my house. I caught a glimpse of this police officer once or twice out of a year, but that was it.

I was still upset over the necklace disappearance. Sniper boy and his girlfriend even screamed at me about this a couple of times. They were angry and I was depressed. I started going out to this restaurant to watch bands play—a favorite past time of mine—and this time started drinking, really drinking, drinking because I was depressed drinking. One night when I was there I saw my cop neighbor and his wife sit down at a table near me. I was on my third or fourth drink and he kept watching me. When he noticed me looking at him, he moved to block my view of his face. Now I saw the back of his head—the view I was used to. Not being able to ever see him was unnerving. I managed to get home safely, but the drinking alone continued...for two years. I was not happy.

Then peculiar things started to happen. I would be driving around town and for no reason a police car would follow me. It looked like the younger cop who was involved in the necklace case. He was cute. I had let him into my house to show him where I thought I had left the necklace. He seemed to be nice, had strong cologne, was flirting with me. Did he like me? Maybe I'll fall in love, too. Get married. Stay in this house I loved and live a normal life, but this police car kept following me—everywhere! I was getting angry. This was not fun. Recognized, noticed, and, followed, and it appeared to be this cop all the time. Was this my imagination? Was I paranoid? Psychotic? Was it real? Or maybe all of the above? I did not know the answer, but I knew it made me angry.

The following me continued or so I thought. I would drive to my shore house—a two hour trip—and a car would follow me. It would be right on my ass, chasing me, swerving in and out. It looked like this cop boy again. I became a very nervous driver. Already driving the speed limit, I began to cautiously drive slower, below the speed limit, maybe dangerously slow for highway driving. I was just nervous. The chasing game was not fun. Right on my ass, swerve very close to others, and then right on my ass again throughout town down to my shore house. I was a wreck. One time when I was driving I stopped by the State Police to report this reckless driving behavior. I exclaimed he was a cop and I was a nervous wreck. The officer asked me for my license which he photocopied and for my license plate number. He warned me not to speed and I was back on the road again.

Now every police officer knows me and my car. Up and down the Garden State Parkway I would be watched by the State Police and tracked. It has been three years, dozens of times up and down the Parkway, and still no tickets. But what have I done? I told the State Police I was being followed by a cop who I thought was harassing me. Was this real?

Then the gun shots began to occur. I would be outside of my house working on my pottery and I'd hear a gun shot. At first I thought it was a firecracker, but it was always one single shot. I thought it was this cop boy again scaring me. So what did I do? The most logical thing to do? I reported it. The police officer said maybe they were hunting. I told him you cannot hunt in my area. This cop knew me. They all did. And he knew where I lived. There was no hunting there. So he took me out of the police station and talked to me about this away from everyone else. I was confused.

So life went on for me—scared and all. Then came ski season at Mountain Creek and this cop boy was still following me or so I thought! I was stressed. I was trying my best to learn how to be a ski instructor, meet my new co-workers, and, most importantly, stay sane. It was not working.

The ski season came to an end. I surprisingly taught skiing successfully, improved my own skiing, and got along well with my fun, talented co-workers. Then the following summer I was going down to the shore and I would finally be away from the harassing town. I needed to take a break from all the madness. I needed to be at the beach relaxing.

Let me backtrack, rewind to sometime, I am not sure when. Actually, I have no idea. I don't remember. At some point I was hospitalized. I went down to the town police department because I thought this cop boy was following me—everywhere. I screamed out of frustration, throwing my keys, and they handcuffed me—really hard. A person without a uniform on jumped out of the hallway, helped the female cop handcuff me, and then he jumped back into the hallway. They put me in a room where they proceeded to photograph me. I was angry. They handcuffed me to a chair and I waited. I had to tell them that I had an illness and what medication I was taking. I had to give them my psychiatrist's phone number. They left me in the room alone. They told me they called my psychiatrist and he said I should be hospitalized. My psychiatrist never said that to them. So this young cop and another cop drove me to the psychiatric hospital for an evaluation. They put me in shackles saying I would be able to walk better. I was humiliated. The evaluation went fine, but the cops told the hospital if I was not admitted they would have to charge me. The social worker then gave me a gown to put on and here I was to stay. The cop returned with my keys and left laughing. I was miserable—mistreated and miserable.

I had to sit contained in a room alone for a few hours. Finally, they came in to get me and put me into a wheelchair and brought me to the psychiatric unit. I listened to a woman repeatedly call the President for those days, heard people confess to taking drugs, and won all the mental health games in the recreational groups. I finally called my parents who were worried about me and told them where I was. Three days later, I was released and my parents came to get me. The psychiatrist did not change my medicine or add anything. I remained the same just even angrier, confused, and hurt.

Somewhere in my crazy life my father was diagnosed with cancer. This was the most awful, unfair, devastating illness I have ever witnessed. I loved my dad and that's all I really know.

The illness crept up on him and my family slowly. It really did not seem to affect him. Well, he did not let it affect him. He went for chemotherapy treatments and actively engaged in his life. He continued to practice as an architect, continued his activities of sailing and golfing, and continued socializing with friends. He seemed to be coping so well. Eventually he had to have surgery. The surgery seemed to be a success. We were all hopeful. He was hopeful. We thought my dad would be okay. He wasn't. The doctor told us he had four to six weeks to live. From that day, my father lived six weeks.

True or not, I was crazy at the time. I was an anxious, paranoid mess. My hospitalizations continued. I was now being hospitalized for panic attacks. I thought I would hear gun shots outside my house and then I'd call the police in my parents' hometown for everything. One time I was letting my dog outside and heard a noise coming from the bushes across the street. Once again, I called the police about me being nervous to let my dog out at night. I was a fucking wreck.

I hated seeing my father die. It was, by far, the worst experience of my life. He became so thin, so weak, and so quickly. It was awful. We tried our best to care for him at home and we did until he died. I have never hated an illness or hated life more. This was unfair. Seeing a person with such a strong personality deteriorate was heartbreaking. Everyone died.

I'm still alive so I really shouldn't complain, but the CIA got involved in the "case" or so I thought. Every undercover cop involved in this harassment case wore a blue shirt so I could distinguish them from others. After all, they were on my side. Scared for my life I was a nervous wreck. It all does not make sense, but it kind of does, doesn't it? Okay, maybe, just maybe, it doesn't.

I savor moments of clarity: moments where a sentence inside my brain makes sense, where I make sense, and when I make sense to others. I want a life of clarity. I want to be free of depression, of mania, of paranoid delusions, of anxiety. I want peace.

I left town when my father died. It was too difficult to pay the rent so I moved back home. My world I created was gone and maybe for the better. I was glad to be at home keeping my mother company. It felt good to be there for her. Psychotic and all, my mom still loved me.

I continued to see the CIA. They were very inconspicuous, but they were there. They followed me out to the bar. I've learned to drink water now. After all, cops are following me and I don't want to drink and drive. And, also, I'm supposed to be an athlete not an alcoholic.

I moved into my family's house down at the New Jersey Shore. If my memory serves me correctly, I remember going to the beach and swimming. And people were still following me! That cop boy, of course, was definitely following me. I saw him on the beach with friends. I tried to confront him, but he walked away. The CIA was there, too. They saw him as well and kept notes on his appearances. See, I'm not crazy; the CIA was working for me. I took pictures of the cop boy with his friends. They followed me everywhere.

One night when I was taking a shower I left the front door unlocked and someone entered and stole my phone. The proof of the pictures of them on the beach was gone now. Now I can't show the judge anything. I had no evidence for my court case. Did I mention I went to the county prosecutor's office to report this police department? They said they would investigate the situation. That's when the CIA got involved or so I thought. Anyway, my pictures were gone so I now I did not have any proof. Maybe the CIA took photos, too.

Did I mention the town police also followed me to Alabama for my cousin's wedding? Yeah, they did—right to the airport and on the plane. It was very stressful. They also made it to my father's funeral as well. That got me angry again.

How does one live with all this going on? There were jets, too. That was the air force tracking this cop boy down and keeping me safe. I heard them every night before I went to bed. They knew what time I went to bed as well and were always protecting me. One time when I was swimming in the ocean a boat came too close to me speeding by. This police department was trying to kill me now! They were angry that the CIA knew about their crimes. Would I be safe? Would I survive? Who would win? I can't even walk my dog at night anymore.

My father was a great architect. He designed beautiful houses, churches, and schools. When he was sick it was obvious he could not work anymore. I had never seen my father cry, but not working devastated him. His whole profession was gone because of an illness. His architecture was who he was: his identity, his love.

Did I mention they followed me to New York City? I went there so the CIA would track me and see all these lunatics following me, chasing me down. Or maybe they were just other cars. But one night they did follow me again. They were at karaoke at the bar. They sang "Pretty woman" to me and "She will be loved." They were nice to me that night. They were always watching out for me.

I like this café. I can have lunch, drink my coffee, and write. No one bothers me. I don't see the CIA or those town police officers. Since the police officers would wear regular clothes while they followed me it was sometimes difficult to know who was who, but I always seemed to figure it out. But the people are nice here in the café. The kids are cute with their parents having lunch. Kids: I love children; but, at the rate I am going, there will never be any children in my future. After all, I can barely function when symptomatic.

Did I mention the Starbucks trap? I always went there to read. That is when I was able to read—not being distracted by the harassing police department. They always came into Starbucks to follow me. They all had shaved heads: skin heads. It was a rough group and they were always angry at me, but at least the CIA was there protecting me.

After my father died and my summer at the beach, I decided to return to Mountain Creek for the winter to work as a ski instructor. Regardless of being psychotic in my first year, they rehired me. That was nice of them.

I was living at a hotel having rented a room for the winter months. That worked out well, but that police department was still following me! It was alright, though, because the CIA was staying at the hotel as well to protect me. Some even got jobs working there. It's a very stressful life, and, meanwhile, I have to give sane, logical ski lessons, and, somehow, I did. I felt okay because the CIA and the jets were keeping me safe. Thank you, Mr. President.

I want to die. I really do. Who wants to live with these thoughts, these emotions, and these experiences? But I'm coming out alive...I think.

My second ski season went surprisingly well. Well, actually, I don't remember it too well due to the CIA and harassment. I was too stressed; however, I do remember passing a ski exam.

PSIA, otherwise known as the Professional Ski Instructors of America, were coming to Mountain Creek and we were encouraged to get our Level 1 certification. The exam included two assessments: one on your skiing ability and one on instructing. I did my best to ignore the CIA and police harassers—they were all skiing by now. The harassers were following me making it dangerous for me to ski and the CIA was following them keeping me safe. Somehow I passed the exam! I did something and I did it well! This was amazing.

That season the Winter Olympics were on TV. I thought I would compete in the Olympics as well: downhill skiing. I could do it, couldn't I? Needless to say, I continued instructing at Mountain Creek and worked on my skiing. Not quite Olympic quality, but it was something. I doubt I'll make it to the Olympics, but the CIA would follow me there as well protecting me from harm, wouldn't they? I thought so.

After my second ski season ended, once again I lived at my shore house for the summer. I went to the beach almost daily and swam as much as I could. I might have done some pottery as well; I'm not quite so sure. My sister and my nephew were spending the summer there, too. I remember teaching Charlie how to throw on the potter's wheel which he loved. I remember because I have pictures of him. No one was watching me or following me that day; well, into my garage studio at least. That was obvious.

Some days I want to go back to the prosecutor's office and ask if they found anything on this police department: organized crime, anything. But I haven't. I'm afraid they will question me, see I'm crazy, and, well, you know, arrest me again, hospitalize me, and I hate hospitals. Whether or not I should be in them; I hate them.

The following winter I found a small apartment in New York to rent for the ski season. I had comforted myself after my father's death by adopting a dog, Darcy. Together we moved into this apartment with my fourteen year old calico cat, Mittens. Despite still being scared at night we were a happy family and New York was good to me. The police in this town were nice—no problems.

Two police officers just walked into this café where I am writing. What do they want now? Are they watching me? Seeing if I'm sane? They have guns, handcuffs. Do they believe me? Do they know or are they just coming in to eat? Anxiety. Paranoia. Does it ever end? The officers are sitting down now. I don't think I can get in trouble for writing, can I? I'll just keep my mouth shut. Are they cute? Of course they are! I better stop looking or else they will question me, maybe even bring me to a hospital. Head down. Just write. Stay out of trouble. I'm still crazy.

There's got to be some sort of drug that stops all of this, isn't there? I already take a mood stabilizer, an antipsychotic, and an antidepressant. I'm tired of popping pills. It's been fifteen years of taking medication. Sometimes it works, sometimes it doesn't. The powerful brain can be so difficult to control.

The cops seem to be ignoring me. Maybe they are intentionally ignoring me. Or maybe they don't even know that I'm the girl who panics, calls the police, gets hospitalized, and repeats the cycle.

My last ski season instructing at Mountain Creek was probably the most successful thus far. I skied better and I instructed sanely. No one seemed to follow me. I didn't even see the CIA! I definitely remained focused on my job. My only anxiety was towards the stressful, busy weekends, but I pulled through. My co-workers were all very nice to me. I became a better skier, a better instructor. Everything went well. For the most part I was healthy, well, healthier. Physically I was a good weight and mentally not too insane. It worked. I worked. It was all good, all very good.

The café cops seem to be ignoring me. I'm out of any trouble, aren't I? I want to ask them if they know of me or have heard of the situation, but I don't. If I hear them say "no" then maybe I can believe that it's all untrue. I really don't think they know me and it's all probably untrue. I think I deserve another summer at the beach. Maybe making art and relaxing for the summer will be good.

Do you think the CIA tracks my phone calls, my text messages, and my internet accounts? Can they see how I spend my money, what I do, all the time? I thought so, but lately there has been no proof, always no proof. The cops are leaving. They seem uninterested in me. That's a relief! And I kept my mouth shut thank goodness—no problems today! Time to go shopping!

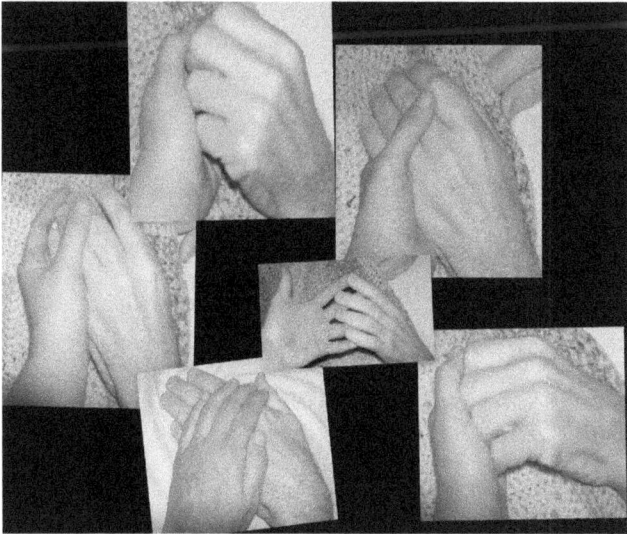

Barbara Arner

8. The Child

I try to let the sadness and anger pass, the hurt, and get on with life. I want to have some meaningful transformation, but it is hard to escape the only mind you have. So I try to write and make sense and bring peace to my troubled existence. I try.

As of lately, I don't think the CIA have been following me. I don't think they listen to my phone calls, read my texts, or see my internet accounts. Lately things seem pretty quiet: peaceful. Why did I have to go through all that? It sounds crazy to the sane mind. It is. It must be.

So I go on. I make pottery, take my dog up to the beach, spend time talking to my mother, and still nothing happens. Life becomes boring. Maybe boring is good. It quiets my mind; lets me focus; brings peace to everything. Maybe the barking dog and the unruly child are not for me, after all. Maybe all I can handle is the stillness, the quiet, the peacefulness of sanity. Every time I experience stress in my life, like my father dying, I get sick. Maybe children are too stressful. Maybe they're not for me.

Life just makes me sad; sad I see everyone going on, not struggling with their thoughts—those demons. People are just easily going about their day and so I get depressed. Can it all fucking end? Please, God, let it end.

The little girl just got up from the table across from me in the café where I am writing and smiled. I smile back. I like children, I really do, but maybe they are not for me. I think I am enough for myself. The trials and tribulations of life; we all have something, don't we?

Isn't life somewhat out of your control? The little girl started to talk to me and asked me what I was writing. I tell her "a book." She told me about her writing experiences in school and that she loves writing as well. She asked if I wanted to have it published, and I said "maybe." See, I'm not crazy all the time. That was a sane conversation, wasn't it?

That meeting and chat with the young child was out of my control and went well. Maybe there is hope. Maybe fate will someday be on my side, just maybe.

The little girl asked what the title was and I told her. She said maybe she'll read it. She asked what it was about. "Life—my life." I'd feel awful if this sweet, little, innocent girl had to read my book filled with such chaotic, crazy stuff. Wow—another sane conversation. Good for me! Thank you, girl, for giving me some hope.

I've had more sane conversations with children. All the children that I taught skiing to this year were endless talkers. I love that children have such freedom when it comes to language during a single ski lesson. I hear their hopes, their dreams, what they love. They are so free, so uninhibited, saner than I, but I manage to give them a good lesson, they learn to ski, and we have fun. And they are so full of life, have so much energy, boundless. I love kids. I really do.

The little café girl just asked me about my calendar on my table here as I write. We chatted about calendars. So free. I love it—talking about anything on their minds. She asked me how many pages I was going to write. "100, maybe." She seemed to approve. Why can't I be a child? My brain would be so…uncluttered. My life would be so…untouched. So free. To be a child.

Barbara Arner

9. The Overachiever

You may not believe this after all I have been through, but I like who I am. I have a nice personality, I'm a good person, and I enjoy my creative talents. Even though it can be difficult at times, I take care of myself. I take responsibility for my illness and treat it the best way I know how. I am not a complete failure. Of course, there are things I can improve upon just like everyone else may desire, but I am pretty content, pretty hopeful.

Where did all this come from? From learning, from taking the time to understand, from being patient, from growing.

Just because it's "not supposed to be this way" doesn't mean it's entirely a curse. By being in therapy for fifteen years, I have come to know myself better and have come to make healthy decisions about my life. I have followed my passions and have pursued art. I've seen my talents evolve and that is rewarding. It gives me personal satisfaction. I constantly strive for self-improvement. I may not be able to achieve it all the time, but it keeps me going. It keeps me alive, and, oh yes, I've kept myself alive throughout everything. That is definitely an accomplishment. As a result of taking care of myself, this time around I eat healthy and exercise more. It's not all lost; some things are okay.

Accepting things you cannot control: it is my life's lesson. Learning to live with an illness and remaining hopeful. It is not always easy at times, but it is possible.

I guess we're all on some sort of path filled with rocks and hills and ruts of all kinds, and, hopefully, filled with sunshine and beautiful views. I hope so. I'm not sure when or if ever, but I remain hopeful.

Maybe all that matters is that I am alive. I have the free will every day to do as I choose: to wake up, to sleep, to make art, not to make art, to see my family and friends, to isolate myself. Maybe it all doesn't matter, but it does. Every word, action, and event matters. Every thought. It does matter. It may not make a whole lot of sense, but it matters. It matters because it is my life, my journey, my only life.

I'm glad I have my dog. Darcy brings me happiness. Mittens does, too, but Darcy makes me laugh with her cute antics. She has to sleep with her head on my pillow every night. Comfortable for her, I guess, comforting for me. I like that there is something out there that I am taking care of; something I love and who loves me in return. It sounds so simple: to love and be loved in return. Unconditionally. Darcy and I. Mittens, too. And today was a good day. The CIA did not follow me. Clear, coherent thinking: what more can I ask for?

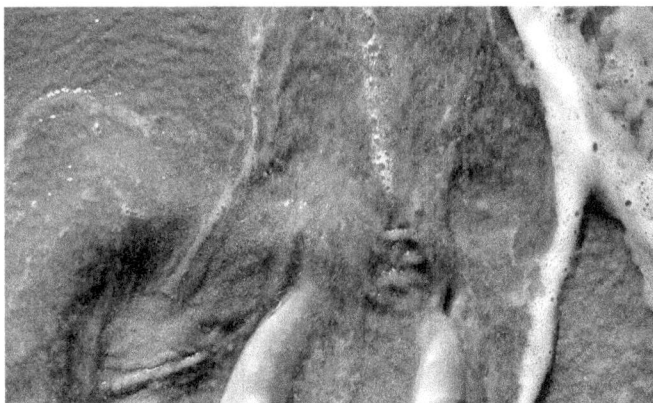

Barbara Arner

10. The Shopper

There's got to be a better life out there for me. There has to. It is just how I feel today. I don't want to eat the vegetables or do the exercise. I want to stay in bed. Why is it such a fight? Am I the problem? The CIA are not following me; I'm just depressed. I just cannot take care of myself again, and, once again, my poor psychiatrist has to dig me out. This sucks. No energy to even write even though writing makes me feel better. How can this life make me happy? Will I feel okay again? I better make myself happy; I don't want to screw up my life. Shopping—I think I'll go shopping.

Barbara Arner

11. The Babysitter

This book has once again become my savior. Thank you, book, for getting me out of bed and getting me somewhere even if it is only straight up with a pen and paper, but doing something: writing.

Today I babysat my nephew Charlie. We had fun playing outside, riding bikes, walking in the woods with the dog, baking cookies, having a sword fight, playing cars, and watching a movie. He kept me going. I was up and then I left, and went down, but then I remembered the book that needs to be written and a life that needs to be lived. But how? How do I live my life? Thirty-four years old. How many years do I have left? How many more do I have to go? How many more is my psychiatrist going to be there for me? How will it be? How will it end? Will I live? Actually live? Like do things with my life that are fulfilling? Fill my life with happiness? What can make me feel happier? Love. Yes, love: a kind, sensitive, caring, understanding, mature love. Is that asking too much? Is it really? One true love? I hope it may exist. Maybe, just maybe, one time it will last and be for real. Maybe for once I'll get myself together; keep myself together.

I enjoyed taking care of Charlie today. We had fun and it went smoothly. I think if I were a parent I could do it. Well, maybe I shouldn't judge an entire lifetime commitment of parenting on one day, but, my point is, I enjoyed taking care of Charlie today and it went well. It was actually easy. It made me go. It made me move forward. I liked it. Amazing what you can learn in six hours of babysitting.

But still there's always so much work to be done. The mind falls apart, the body falls apart. The mind comes together, the body comes together. I feel like there is a constant fight within me, a constant struggle, always striving for inner peace: calm, no worries. I want to be free from everything: free from depression, from mania, from psychosis, from anxiety, from normal personality issues. Time to make another phone call to the psychiatrist and he always answers, weekends, weeknights, he answers. He puts in overtime for this brain, all the time.

But today I managed to babysit Charlie and I did it well. He was like a little antidepressant—bursts of fun, bursts of energy. "Is it always like that, so easy and manageable?" asks the six-hour babysitter. I need to feel better all the time: my wish, my hope, my dream come true. It's like wanting to be in love all the time—to have those good chemical feelings—all the time. This face of mine should be smiling much more than it has been. Sometimes I cannot even remember the last time I laughed or smiled.

Why do you keep on listening? Why do you keep on reading? I'm afraid nothing will change, improve, evolve, or aspire. "Why even bother?" says the depressed mind. "Continue!" says the determined one. Finish something that brings you joy, that fills you with happiness, sadness, anger, hurt, pain, and love: a book of pain and love.

Babysitting Charlie today got me out of myself. It got me moving in a forward direction. We were busy. He kept me busy. He kept me active. I kept him safe and let him have fun. We played, explored, relaxed, and created. He wasn't too interested in my spelling lessons, but as a four year old what can you really expect? We had more fun playing with toys and our imaginations.

I miss my father. I wish he were here to see his family grow, to see his grandchildren, not die from cancer, the most awful, devastating disease that exists, killing my dad, taking his life so quickly, in so few weeks, leaving him so frail, so weak, so sick. Fuck you, illness. I love you, Dad. I miss you dearly. I promise I'll stay out of bed as much as I can for you. Stop wasting away the days. As you always said to me, "As long as you tried your best." And I always do try my best. If I did not try my best I would be cheating myself, not being true to who I am, and, therefore, failing. No matter how small the task I am trying my best, Dad. Isn't it nice that I had such a great day with Charlie? He was so sweet, so well-behaved, and it was so easy. I'm actually proud of myself for babysitting him so well. It was really nothing ground-breaking in the history of babysitting, but it was nice, nice to know there was something that could keep me going and that I did well.

My ninety-seven year old aunt just passed away. A day before she died I told her I wish my father were alive to see us. She said he was watching down on us. She always had such a strong faith. Aunt Muriel. I loved her. I love how she loved me. I loved our relationship. I've never told someone how much I loved them before their death like I told her; how awful and painful death can be.

But today Charlie was sunshine. And Darcy was playful. And the bike ride was fast. And the cookies were yummy. And movie time was snugly. And our lunch outside was peaceful. It was a perfect day. It really was. Thank you, Charlie.

Barbara Arner

12. The Crafter

I am participating in a craft show now and it is slow. There are people wandering and browsing, but it is slow. Cloudy today, but the festival is taking place in a nice park. Thirty-six artists and crafters showed up with tents and set-up and here I am with my two tables and pottery. I have a view of the river and the people are nice and I am out of bed. I almost stayed in bed. In fact, I woke up, had breakfast, and then went back to bed for thirty minutes. Then after much self-talk, I got myself together, and here I am. People are looking at my artwork and giving me nice compliments and it feels good.

Pottery is really no way to make a living, it really isn't. Maybe I should have done something else with my life. Like what: a lawyer, a doctor? Not for me. Pottery is fun. A messy, fun time, but poor, very poor. What is Plan B? Thoughtless. A ski instructor is Plan B and that is tiring work. Three years down. How many more to go? Last season was my best season instructing. I had a good handle on it. The kids were fun to work with. Maybe I'm just getting older. Maybe my zest for living is deteriorating. I don't know why. Maybe I'm just...depressed. If I were talking to my psychiatrist he would be saying good things about me. I can't seem to think of any. Did I take the antidepressant this morning? Yes, I did. Who would have thought?

My pottery loves just sitting here staring at me. Should I just pack you up now, sweet pottery? I'm glad I'm writing my book. Plan B or is that Plan C? Or no plan at all? Planless. But I love making art. I may be pathetically poor, but I love the art process, just like writing. I just wonder if anything goes anywhere at some point. Maybe I'm doing something wrong. Maybe I'm doing a lot of things wrong. I did get out of the bed this morning.

The craft fair ended and the people were nice. No one bought anything, but I was out of my bed so I was happy. So it actually was a successful day, a very successful day.

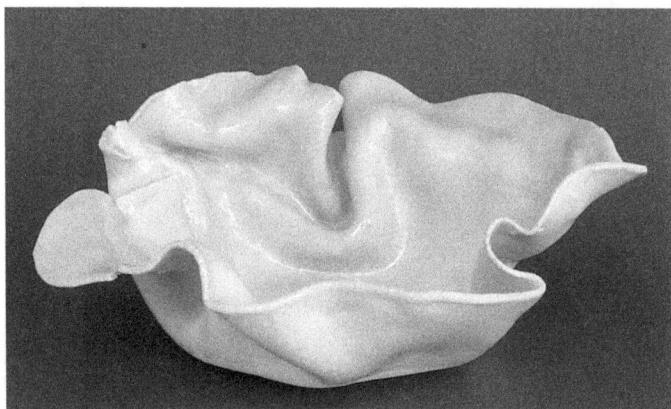

Barbara Arner

13. The Judge

Since I thought everyone was following me there was obviously going to be a lawsuit. I would sue everyone for harassing me and I would win. Justice would be served. They would do some jail time, my thoughts and experiences would be validated, and I would heal. Well, no lawsuit has occurred, and, to the best of my knowledge, no one has been following me as I sit in this coffee house a cop walks in. He doesn't make eye contact, simply gets his coffee, pours in some milk, and then leaves. Does he know that I'm the girl who has been calling the cops on the cops? Is he aware of all this or did he just want a cup of coffee? He probably just wanted a cup of coffee as my mind gets jumbled. Fucking illness. Fucking life. Fucking day. What happened to peacefully writing the book in the coffee house? Maddening yet again.

As I was saying, a lawsuit has not evolved and as it appears the only one who is guilty, the only one who is crazy, the only one who is to blame, is, well, me. Maybe this illness is all I can handle, after all. Maybe that is the truth. Maybe having a dog, a cat, and artwork to make is enough for me. Maybe I ought to keep it simple. This manic, racing mind is complex enough. To add to it might bring more insanity. Why me? Really, God, why me? Why give something difficult to someone for their entire lifetime? I don't get it. I really don't. A mental illness does not bring happiness. It brings pain, sadness, disappointments, hurt, and exhaustion. It's not fair. It will never be and I hate it so I bitch and complain and whine and cry and who is to blame? Who is guilty? Who's mind gets messy all the time? Who has to deal with nonsense? Who has to be in therapy weeding out this and that coming to the truth? Who has to come to terms with a disillusioned reality? Who is guilty? Me, me, and me. All the time: me. Did you know that, Mr. Police Officer? Did you know that I'm the one who calls the cops on everything? That I'm the paranoid one? Did you know that only I'm guilty or were you just getting your coffee? I hope you were just getting your coffee, but I'm sure you knew.

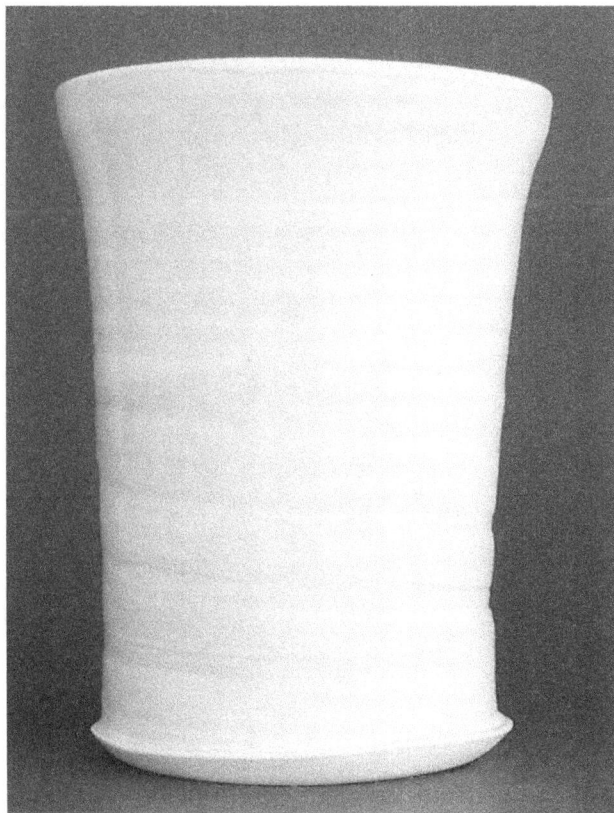

Barbara Arner

14. The Optimist

I believe in life, love, and the pursuit of happiness. I really do. I strive for it and sometimes I feel it. It is not always so tragic. I have supportive, caring family and friends who love me. I am able to live by the beach and create art. My parents have provided me with love, comfort, and security. I have a quiet, peaceful life, yes, with an unexpected illness, but I am surviving and maybe thriving. Living by the beach creates a life of tranquility; it gives me peace of mind. I love taking walks on the beach or just sitting looking out into the waves. Staring at the never-ending waves, losing myself in the water, in the repetitive sound, the salty air, the sandy beach. I love it all while calming this raging mind.

Barbara Arner

Barbara Arner

15. The Potter

I'm not sure when in high school I heard of the profession of an art therapist, but I knew it was my dream job, my educational goal. My interest in combining art and psychology into a helping profession was what I wanted to do with my life.

After attaining my Bachelor's degree in studio art and psychology, I planned to continue my education to obtain a Master's degree in counseling psychology and art therapy. Finally, the tuition would be worth every penny and I would have a profession, be able to support myself, and all would be great—wishful thinking. Toss bipolar into the mix and life gets a little tortured. I was unable to finish my graduate degree due to the intensity of my illness, but I enjoyed every minute of my brief art therapy experience. I loved my classes and I loved working with the patients. Even though my art therapy career did not evolve, I became a potter and a pottery teacher. Art, instead, healed me.

The art process transforms you. My father, an architect, never spoke of the process, but I am sure he loved what the creative process did for him. He was passionate about his profession. It consumed him and for someone as talented, devoted, and passionate as he was it was no wonder that he was so successful. He was a skilled artist able to draw, paint, and, ultimately, design. His finished buildings were all beautiful and always a complex process I could never comprehend. He was my father and I was proud of him and all that he could do. I am sure this creative art process brought much joy and satisfaction into his life and I can only see and think that because that is what I, too, have experienced.

I love pottery. I love how clay feels: how it is a soft, smooth, beautiful material, yet fun and messy to play with, but it is the process that transforms. I've cried, laughed, smiled, paused, thought, relaxed, screamed, gotten angry more times than I can remember, and it has always healed me; made me feel better. As a result, I have always made something: a bowl, a plate, a vase, sculpture. I can choose my clay color, usually white, and select from an unlimited amount of colorful glazes. I've mastered the art of firing a kiln and can successfully pot on the potter's wheel. I have been on this journey making pottery for fourteen years now...art heals.

Barbara Arner

16. The Psychotic

A friend asked me once if I knew when I was psychotic. I did not know how to answer. I thought, "Of course I do not know I'm psychotic. Why on earth would I be doing all the things I am doing?" Then another part of me thought, "Yes, I know, I just cannot stop the thoughts that are making me delusional." I think both answers are true.

Bipolar disorder with psychotic features: my mental illness. I experience bipolar mood swings from mania to depression and I am also one of the lucky ones who has psychotic episodes: my delusions or false thoughts that destroy my fragile reality. I also tend to get paranoid and anxious so that can thus be added into the diagnosis. I keep my psychiatrist and myself quite busy.

I wish all these problems would just disappear, but they never will. Maybe they will be less frequent, maybe not. Maybe they will be less intense, maybe not. All I know to do is take my medication and see my psychiatrist regularly to keep everything at bay: increasing my medication when the symptoms begin and decreasing it when they subside until the next episode. It's hard work, my full-time job taking care of myself, and sometimes I succeed and sometimes I fail.

Psychosis is challenging because it feels so real. Who would not believe their thoughts? Well, when you are psychotic it's best not to believe one thought and thoughts are so powerful that you can act on them; these false thoughts then become your reality. For me, this makes bipolar disorder unbearable and sometimes unlivable.

I think I got married twice already. I don't have a ring on my finger or a husband by my side, but I got married. I really did—twice. Once I was on the beach in a pink sundress waiting for him to show up. I was ready. He never showed up. I went home and saw my psychiatrist instead. Another time I was really getting married. This time I even secretly purchased the wedding dress, and, of course, had it fitted, too. There wasn't a set date or a husband waiting by my side this time either (no proposal for that matter), but I was ready. It was going to be a beautiful wedding. It took me a while to decide on my bridesmaids' dresses let alone the bridesmaids. After much delusional thinking, I decided I would just have my sister as my maid-of-honor (I was going to let her choose her own dress). I was not quite sure if my husband-to-be would be okay with just a best man. I hoped it would be alright. It was difficult to know because he wasn't really, well...there. So a few pieces were missing to my planned wedding, but the dress looked pretty and everyone at the bridal store wished me well.

Sometimes the delusions seem so real that they tinker daily with your life. This can be both frustrating and exhausting, but today no one has been following me which makes it a very nice, quiet, peaceful day. Even though no one did follow me, though, it does not mean that they could not have. Today I went to the beach alone. Being alone is always dangerous because people could follow me, strangle, and kill me. My mom would be devastated, but no one followed solo me to the beach. I managed to stay on the quiet beach with a sense of peace and tranquility and amazingly enjoy my afternoon: another accomplishment. It was nice. I sat on the beach, put my feet in the water, and listened to the crashing waves; and no one murdered me.

Barbara Arner

17. The Grown-up

I was driving in stop-and-go traffic on the Garden State Parkway the other day, and began to follow the car's lead in front of me and slowly stop. Then a loud "crash" and I went propelling forward and halted to a stop: rear-ended.

I got out of my car to see both the other driver first, the cars second. He was already on the phone and did not appear to be hurt. His car was wrecked and not drivable and my bumper was dented. We were okay.

Within minutes a police officer showed up and directed us where to pull over. I did not panic. I did not cry. I did not scream, lose my temper, or whine. I did not complain, argue, or do anything negative. The officer handled the accident quickly and easily.

I was glad the police officer handled the car accident the way he did. There was no questioning my sanity or my state of mental health. There was no reason to. There were no mental health issues, insane behaviors, or questionable acts. I even had a coherent thought to describe the accident to the officer. I handled a stressful situation with my illness and I was okay. This was definitely a good day for a car accident. I never made it to the ceramic store for my pottery supplies, but I was okay both mentally and physically and that's all that mattered. It was a good day—a great day, actually.

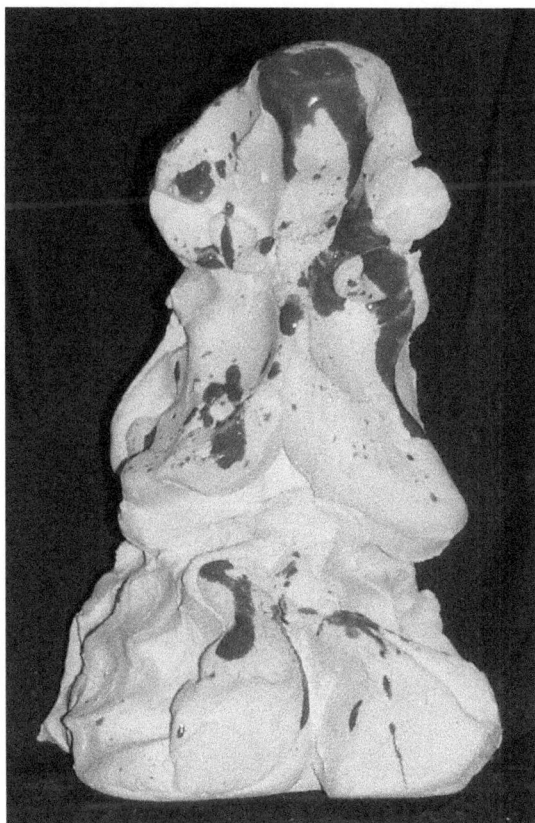

Barbara Arner

18. The Survivor

The experience of having psychotic delusions, having your world shaken, turned upside-down and inside-out, would disturb anyone. Going through these experiences is what makes me want to kill myself. My daily life gets disrupted, I cannot work, and I cannot function. I buy wedding dresses, after all. I know these periods are temporary, but they exist and it is upsetting. My family gets confused, my friends do not fully understand, my psychiatrist has to work overtime, and I am off believing everything that is untrue.

I am not really sure anymore what world I live in more often: a delusional one or one based on reality. Delusions are so believable and I cannot have my psychiatrist following me around correcting every little thought I have. I am left daily to my own devices to decipher what is real, what is not, and what is going to be done about everything. Echoing in my mind during these times is the repetitive, "killing yourself is not an option." My belief in this statement wavers. Sometimes it is a strongly held belief, other times I have to convince myself that it is, well, really not an option. So that means living and living with all of this: a life without total control, a life that was chosen for me, a life of challenges, of some accomplishments. Redefining what it means to be successful. Just to make it through another day. To live another day is to succeed. To survive.

Barbara Arner

Barbara Arner

19. The Dog Walker

I love my dog. She is one of the purchases I do not regret and having her has brought me pure joy.

I adopted Darcy from a humane shelter approximately a year ago. She was found on the side of the road and was brought into the shelter by the police (the same police officers who I have repeatedly called for help). She had the parvovirus and they did not know if she would survive. She, too, survived. At three months she was ready for adoption and that was when I decided I needed something to take care of and to keep me company.

I fell in love with Darcy immediately. She was adorable as a puppy. She had black, soft, fluffy fur and was in constant motion. I wasn't. It was April and since my father had passed away on July 4th, I had become very depressed. I had gained weight and was not doing well. I was moving slowly, but Darcy was jumping around. She had energy. She had life. And I loved her.

Darcy has a wonderful temperament. She is overly friendly and acts as a wonderful protector. She is part Flat-Coated Retriever and part German Shepherd and weighs about forty-five pounds. I think she is beautiful.

When she was young, I took her to puppy kindergarten classes. She loved playing with the other dogs romping around. Keeping her socialized, I continued taking her to dog parks. This also helped me by getting me out of the house and interacting with other dog owners. We were a good match. I continued after her puppy classes with basic obedience. She learned the basics of sit, stay, and come, and learned how to heal. In this class she even earned the blue ribbon out of all the dogs during the final test. I was proud of our efforts and her advancement. She was doing exceptionally well. It was suggested by one of the trainers that she would be a great therapy dog. She also attained her pet therapy and Canine Good Citizen certifications. Darcy was impressive. She went through the classes effortlessly.

Every night Darcy sleeps in my bed and snuggles up against me. It's pure love. I take care of her, she knows it, and she loves me. Loving each other for who we are. Isn't that how simple love ought to be? Darcy and me: my therapy.

Barbara Arner

20. The Thriver

Today: Do whatever I can do and do it the best I can.
Get out of bed
Shower
Shave
Get dressed
Eat a healthy breakfast
Take medicine
Brush teeth
Take the dog for a walk
Make art
E-mail
Listen to music
Read
Write
Exercise
Go to the dog park
Go out to lunch
Eat healthy
See psychiatrist
Cry
Laugh
Listen
Think
Express myself
Talk to friends
Go shopping
Get hair cut
Get a manicure/pedicure
Get a facial
Watch a movie
Take a nap
Cook
Clean
Do laundry
Grocery shop
Do a project or hobby

Do something fun
Eat a healthy dinner
Talk to family members
Relax
Take a bath
Assess my daily mood
Be happy I got through another day
Take my medicine
Get ready for bed
Pray
Be at peace with myself
Go to sleep

Anyone with bipolar disorder knows that it is not enough to survive, you must thrive. You must live your life the best you can: in work, in relationships, in yourself. Even with mental health challenges, you must thrive. You must live. I must live. I must thrive. Psychotic or not, I must live my life the best way I know how.

It has been about a week since I have not been psychotic I am happy to say. I actually even saw two police officers driving up and down my street and both waved to me. It was nice and normal. It made me think and believe that anything, once again, could be possible. I was thinking clearly and I was okay.

I think I'll go make some pottery—in peace.

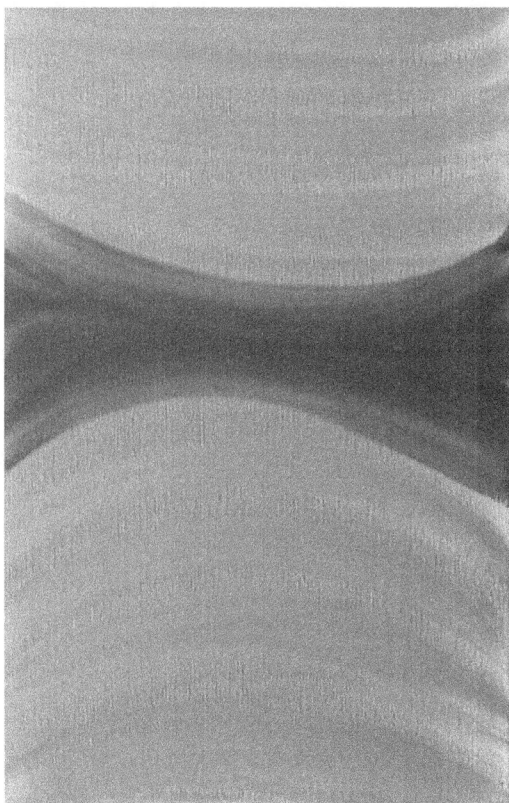

Barbara Arner

21. The Soloist

I think we all need a blank slate sometimes: a new beginning, a better path, feeling renewed, refreshed, rejuvenated.

That is how I feel today. I'm not sure why. Maybe I am finally just giving myself the chance to breathe again, to live again: free from the pain, free from the worry, free from every negative emotion that has consumed me and my first thirty-four years. Letting go of the hurt, anger, and sadness and becoming free from all the negative energy. Continuing to take care of myself the best I can, continuing to live the best I can, and choosing life and letting life choose me. Just letting everything work together well: taking my medicine, going to therapy, and getting out of bed, always getting out of bed.

Why should it take so much effort and energy to be well? So much time? Will it always? Does it get easier? I'm no master of life, but I do think and truly believe that anything is possible: a career, a relationship, a family, love. Whatever you choose, whatever chooses you. I believe it is possible.

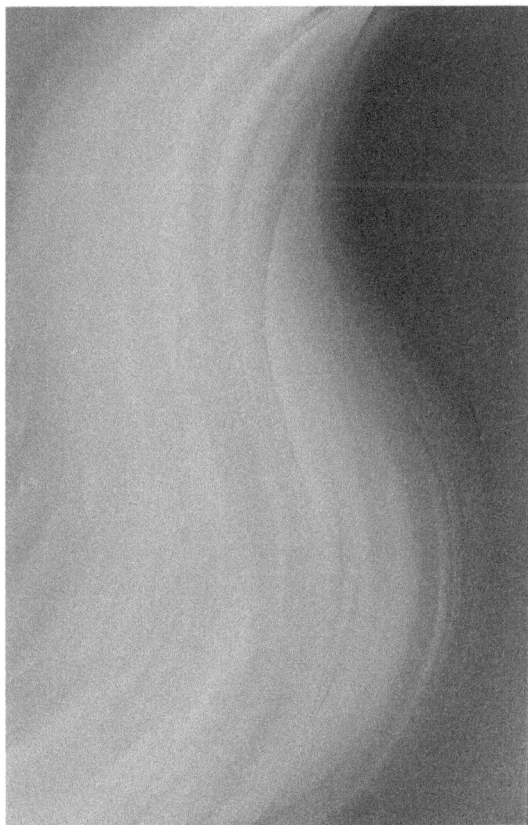

Barbara Arner

22. The Writer

Well, the good news is that I am not psychotic. The bad news is that I am depressed. I really want to be optimistic, upbeat, positive, but that is not how I am feeling, not how I am doing.

I don't want to shower, I don't want to take care of myself, and I don't want to live. Why again? Is it me? Is it the illness? Is it both? I want negative feelings to vanish, to go away, to leave—permanently. I want to feel happy, satisfied, successful, pleasant. I don't.

I am angry—furious. Bleeding anger. Rage. Towards an illness; towards an illness I don't want.

Just get over it, right? I need to learn to just get over a lot of things: get over this illness, get over wanting to be thinner, get over wanting to be loved. Just get over it. Life, feelings, and emotions should be so easy.

Instead I go to therapy. Again, dissatisfied at my life, at myself, at me, with nothing, being nothing, with having to cater to an illness, with being frustrated, with being angry. Why? Because I want a book with a happy ending. I want to be happy like he is, like she is, have what they have, live how they live. I want to do what they do, be able to do what they do. I get so angry. Even I can shrink myself into the right way of thinking, but this is how I feel. And my feelings are strong and they run deep and they are real. And this is my life and I am unhappy.

So what is good about it? What does make me happy? What do I have? What does make life worth living? I really don't know. I would say family and friends, but I really don't communicate deeply with anyone anymore it seems. My friends are involved in their lives with their partners and families, and my brother and sister are involved in their lives. I speak with my mother, but with her I don't want to feel burdensome. Instead, I lead a very isolated life. I know, shrink myself again, "socialize more," "call a friend," "talk to someone." Well, when I don't feel like it, and don't want anyone to see me so depressed, I tend to isolate myself. So it's me, the cat, and the dog. I showered and walked the dog so I get some points, right? Well, maybe that's not enough, definitely not enough. I read, I did an errand, I went out to lunch, and I am writing. I'm getting there, right? More and more and more that makes me feel good, more that makes me feel productive. I did the dishes. I fed my dog. More that makes me feel good. I sold some pottery. More, more, more.

I am supposed to be happy. It is summer, the beginning of summer, by the beach here, and this is how I am feeling. I cannot escape my feelings. I don't know how to. I do not know how to get rid of this anger, hurt, sad, painful feeling. I don't know where to go; what to do. And everything is wrong. I want to stay in bed. I want to sleep. I want to eat. I don't want to exercise. I just don't want to take care of myself. I don't want to.

"But just love yourself," I shrink myself. Love yourself. Be kind to yourself, but I still feel. I still feel angry, hurt, sad, frustrated. Like a bipolar failure: failure in life, love, and the pursuit of happiness. Failure, failure, failure.

I hate writing this. I hate being true to myself. I hate it. I want to be happy and well and well-adjusted. I want to be healthy: healthy all the time. Is that asking too much? Is it really? I'm sure some people go about their lives not ever considering the possibility that they are not healthy. They are functioning, not taking medicine. They are doing fine. I'm sure there are people like that. I know there are. I envy every one of them. I used to be like that before I got sick. They have their health. That is not an area of struggle for them. I know, I shrink myself again, "But we all have problems. No one is perfect." Yeah, I know, but that is how I feel and I am angry that it is such a fight. Furious.

So just accept it, right? I need to accept every damn thing that is wrong with me: accept this damn illness, accept my inadequacies, accept my failures, accept my faults, accept my mistakes, just accept everything. What a mighty struggle living can be. Will it always be like this? Will I always have to cope? Does it get better? Or, for fear, does it get worse?

I really hate being so angry. Here, you have a mental illness, now go live, be happy, and prosper. If it were like that I would be doing much better. I would be surviving and thriving all the time. I wouldn't be struggling. I would prosper. I wouldn't be so angry. Can't all this anger subside once and for all? Please, God, please? Can't it just go away? Just let me live. Let me be happy. Successful. Satisfied. Let me live in peace, in comfort, not struggling to work, not struggling to live. Let something be easy.

I yearn for a sense of control: control over my illness, control over my life. I want control. I want to feel stable, secure, safe. I want something healthy. I want to be healthy. I try, I do, and I fail. Over and over again. The never-ending battle of bipolar disorder: accepting the battle, befriending it, not calling it a battle, but a challenge. Not something to fight with, but something to work with. But you get me so angry. So angry I have to write. So angry I have to cope. So angry all the time. I want to be well all the time. Not angry all the time. I want to feel in control. I want to have control. Mastery. Yes, a sense of mastery over this illness. Yes, I am victorious—I won—I did it! But I haven't. I struggle to live every day. It does not feel like any sense of control or mastery.

I've worked hard on myself. I go to therapy, I take my medicine—for over a decade now. I should be feeling better. I should be doing better. I'm not. Why? Why do I have to be stuck in this cycle? Feeling good, feeling depressed, feeling good, feeling depressed. It gets exhausting. I'm exhausted.

I wish I could write a book of hope, promise, endurance, faith, and love, but it feels like none of the above. It feels like failure. A failed life. Career plans and goals—failed. Relationships—failed. Independence—failed. Everything—failed. Standing still in my life. Not moving anywhere.

Today I did get the basic essentials down. I did well. I got out of bed. I showered. I did errands, took the dog for a walk, but I was so angry, felt so angry it ruined my day. Angry at an illness, angry at life. Angry, angry, angry. Angry all day. A constant feeling. Too angry to quietly and peacefully make pottery. Too angry to want to live. Angry that I'm feeling so angry. Angry now that I have to write the word "angry" so many times. Angry, angry, angry, angry. Therapy, therapy, therapy, therapy.

Angry at hating myself. Angry at being angry. Angry at losing my father. Anger at not having a career. Anger at not living independently. Anger at having to take medicine. Anger at not having any children. Anger at not being successful. Anger that I have to write so much about anger. Anger that no one "gets it." Anger that it is difficult to be successful. Angry, angry, angry. Angry that I feel this way. Angry that I want to die. Angry that this is my reality. Angry that this is it. That this is my life. Angry that this is my life.

A new beginning. Is that possible? Can you start new? What would that be? What would that feel like? What would I do? I would have to live for starters. Have to live. So that means doing things; maybe doing something new. What could that be? What do I want to do? What could make me feel less angry? Lately, it has been reading and walking my dog. Both have made me feel relaxed, calm, at peace. That's probably not the most ground-breaking answer I was looking for, but it is something for starters.

There's got to be hope, right? Hope in what? Hope that I'll live pain-free. Hope that this pain will all go away. Hope that it will not get worse. Hope that things will change. Hope that I will change. Hope that I will get better. Again and again and again and again. Hope that I will feel good. Hope that I will take care of myself. Hope that I can support myself. Hope that I will be okay. Hope that everything will be okay. Hope that I'll be loved. Hope that it's the right love. Hope that I'll survive. Hope that I won't think destructive thoughts. Hope that I'll stay alive. Hope that I can live a happy, healthy, productive life. Happy—doing things I enjoy. Healthy—not getting sick. Productive—contributing to society. Moving forward. Not standing still. Not being so angry anymore. Moving forward into new terrain. Completing a book. Writing. Happiness. Expressing myself. Expressing myself to you. Healing. Feeling better. Feeling good. Writing.

Barbara Arner

23. The Journalist

Being well is not enough. Taking care of myself is not enough. Surviving, then thriving, and, ultimately, living. Laughing. Where did the laughter go? Where did the smiles go? When did all that disappear? When will it return? When will I live? When will life, fate, be good to me? I was good to you, life, wasn't I? I did not do anything wrong; anything hurtful. I did not do anything to deserve pain.

If a mental illness were all so easy we would just take a pill and move on, but it is not so easy; not at all. I want to feel ease, happiness, enjoyment, fulfillment, but those concepts are so foreign to my thoughts, to my life.

Desperately wanting to live. Desperately wanting to live a happy life. Desperate to make this a happy life. Controlling my life for once. Controlling how I want to feel. Not being dictated to by a mental illness. Not wondering if I'm going to stay depressed, become manic, think psychotic thoughts, feel suicidal. I just want normalcy. Plain, boring. Black and white. Normal. That is what I want. None of the extras that come with bipolar disorder. No more headaches. No more dramas. No more lost dreams. Lost hopes. No more nightmares. I want my happy ending. I don't want you, bipolar disorder, I don't want you.

Barbara Arner

Barbara Arner

24. The Contemplator

Bipolar disorder makes you stop and think. It puts you in psychotherapy and you sit and talk and contemplate life; you contemplate yourself. You can't escape. You are left to deal with reality and it never ends.

I've talked about my illness, my friends, my family, and myself over and over and over again. I've talked about my life, my life plans, and my situation. I've laughed, I've cried, I've probably felt every emotion possible, and, not only have I felt it, I've talked about it. Bipolar disorder makes you stop and think.

It halts your life. It makes you question your relationship with others, your relationship with yourself— my relationship with me. It makes me stop and think.

What do I want now? What do I want to do now? Why? With whom? What is best for me? Do these questions matter? What will make me happy? What will make me unhappy? Will I be okay? Will I get sick again? Will I be able to handle my life?

Everything matters. Every thought, every action matters. Every feeling. And how I feel is how I manage to be: to be well, to be sick, to take care of myself, to let myself go. Making these decisions every day. Getting out of bed when all I want to do is stay in bed and sleep. Sleep the day away; sleep my life away; escape the pain. What is worth living? People have kids they love, jobs that fulfill them. I try to figure it all out in therapy. Just do it. Just do something that will work, that will finally make sense. Succeed at something.

Thankfully, I like who I am. After thousands of dollars in therapy, I better like who I am. I like my mannerisms, my personality, my talents, my intelligence. I like myself. I just struggle sometimes and that frustrates me. I struggle with my mind and that makes things difficult. It gets me angry; gets me upset.

I just want to be well. I want to be better. I want to live undisturbed. I don't want to deal with this anymore.

I want to feel something positive. I want to feel positive energy. No more dark, negative depressions. Carefree, loving. Not angry; not hurt; not sad anymore. A new way to feel. Something different. Not delusional anymore. Please delusions, stay away. Please mania, stay away. Please depression, go away. Being safely in the middle. Balanced. Please, God, please? For now? For once? For a while? Wishing away a chemical disorder. It's worth a try, worth a wish, isn't it? Now can you see why it's so easy to give up? Bipolar is just not a fun time. It's not joyous, it's not pleasant, and I don't want it, but I have it, it's mine, and I can either be angry or accept it. So I accept it and get on with life. I try, but, still, it is not easy.

I wish I had someone who would understand and who would tell me that I am doing okay, that I will be okay, that things will get better, and that I will move on. That someone would be there for me all the time, but I am alone. Standing alone. Alone. Alone. Alone. If I were in a relationship it may be nice. I hate when I see people in relationships who are nasty, selfish, or just mean-spirited. Love? What kind of love is that? People deserve understanding, patience, kindness, respect. Love. I may never be in a relationship, but at least I know how people should be treated and loved.

Where did I go wrong? Did I go wrong? Am I just trying to live? Just trying to take care of myself; just trying something; just trying not to give up really. Survive. Thrive. Live.

I want to be victorious. I really do and I try. I try my best every day. I have no choice, but to live. I refuse to kill myself; to give into the feeling; to give up. So I choose to accept an illness I don't want to have, get over it, and get on. Get on with life however that may be. Eat healthy. Take the dog for a walk. Get out of bed.

Do something. Write a book: a therapeutic, personal journey. A time to contemplate. A time to accept. A time to love. A time to love doing something. A time to love me. A time to succeed. A time to succeed at being me. A time to succeed at living.

Barbara Arner

25. The Winner

Keratoconus and all, I can finally see. I can see. I have always been able to see though not clearly. A warped perspective. A tainted view. A view that was mine. A view of my own. How I see; how I feel. My reality. Whether it is right or wrong, just or unjust; it is mine. How I see myself, how I experience the world. My story. A learning experience. A growing experience. A journey.

I'm not sure what lay in front of me, but I know where I have been. I've been through a lot without going very far. Now I am ready to live. To go somewhere. Somewhere inside myself again, somewhere outside myself. Taking my time moving forward. Gaining a better perspective. Learning from my past perspective. Growing. Learning. Changing. Remaining true to myself. Loving myself. Loving others. Always having hope. Being brave. Being strong with all this illness brings; with all that I can offer; offer this world; offer myself. To survive. Thrive. Live. Love. Laugh. Have some fun. Hope. Hope that I will always be okay. Growing. Embracing. Embracing an illness I hated. An illness that once destroyed my life. Accepting bipolar disorder and living. Living and enjoying that life; the only life that I was given. Contributing to others. Contributing to the world. Beginning again. Continuing. Continuing from a new perspective. From a new view. A view of my own.

www.ingramcontent.com/pod-product-compliance
Lightning Source LLC
Chambersburg PA
CBHW031211270326
41931CB00006B/515